WHEN
GOD
IS IN CONTROL

DR. ROSIE GOLDSBY

Edited by Stephanie Malench

WESTBOW
PRESS®
A DIVISION OF THOMAS NELSON
& ZONDERVAN

WestBow Press books may be ordered through booksellers or by contacting:

WestBow Press
A Division of Thomas Nelson & Zondervan
1663 Liberty Drive
Bloomington, IN 47403
www.westbowpress.com
844-714-3454

Because of the dynamic nature of the Internet, any web addresses or
links contained in this book may have changed since publication and
may no longer be valid. The views expressed in this work are solely those
of the author and do not necessarily reflect the views of the publisher,
and the publisher hereby disclaims any responsibility for them.

Any people depicted in stock imagery provided by Getty Images are models,
and such images are being used for illustrative purposes only.
Certain stock imagery © Getty Images.

Scripture quotations marked NIV are taken from the Holy Bible, New
International Version®, NIV®. Copyright © 1973, 1978, 1984 by Biblica,
Inc.™ Used by permission of Zondervan. All rights reserved worldwide.

Scripture quotations marked ESV are from the ESV Bible®
(The Holy Bible, English Standard Version®), copyright ©
2001 by Crossway Bibles, a publishing ministry of Good News
Publishers. Used by permission. All rights reserved.

Scripture quotations marked KJV are taken from
the Holy Bible, King James Version.

Scripture quotations marked NKJV are taken from the
New King James Version. Copyright © 1982 by Thomas
Nelson, Inc. Used by permission. All rights reserved.

ISBN: 979-8-3850-0813-1 (sc)
ISBN: 979-8-3850-0812-4 (e)

Library of Congress Control Number: 2023918186

Print information available on the last page.

WestBow Press rev. date: 10/06/2023

Contents

Introduction

Thank you for reading this page so you can understand why I wrote this book. For many years I believe the Spirit has been telling me to write a book but I would tell Him, I will write plays instead using other character names to discuss things that have gone on in my life. I even told an associate my plays were the same as a book and he would not agree. At this point in my life the Spirit does not agree either.

This book has been written so that I could remember and deal with some of the issues that have happened to me along the way. When I prayed and asked God to let some of those issues not be in the forefront of my mind, I think everything that happened in that time period also was erased. Yes, until I reflected on the bad, I could then remember some of the good things that happened in the same time period.

Maybe some of you have struggled with the call to do spiritual assignments or make career choices and you think you do not have what it takes, think again. This time I want you to repeat what it says in Philippians 4:12-13 (KJV)," I know how to be abased, and I know how to abound: everywhere and in all things, I am instructed both to be full and to be hungry, both to abound and to suffer need. I can do all things through Christ who gives me strength."

I often questioned who needed to know my story. I was afraid to tell my story, share boldly and be content in my circumstances. During this process I have learned to be confident and have joy in God regardless of my weaknesses and trials. Struggles are a part of life, but if God is leading your life, He will provide the comfort and strength you need.

To write this book I had to present my body as a living and holy sacrifice to God which is my reasonable form of worship. I needed to forget about what others may say or think about what I am sharing and to not think more highly of myself than what I should. My desire is to do what is good and is the will of God. Some people will agree and others will not but since God says it is time to write, I know someone will be helped.

In the text of the book, I struggled with using "the voice of the Lord, Holy Spirit, and God" when referring to times when I was urged to move by a spirit other than my own. Because I believe it is one in the same, I feel a freedom to use them interchangeably. Through the years, prayer and fasting helped me to distinguish the voice of God from my own.

I leave you with the prayer from 3 John 1:2 (ESV), Beloved, I wish above all things that you prosper and be in good health even as your soul prospers.

Foreword

Dear Reader,

I am the product of a strong, resilient, anointed, God-fearing woman named Dr. Rosie Goldsby. Her life struggles, failures and successes made her the woman she is today. When God is in Control is not only the title of this book but has been a consistent theme of her life and walk with the Almighty God.

From a young child I witnessed her unique ability to praise God in any situation. She not only taught me about the love and power of God but showed me the benefit of giving my time, talent and tithe to God. I developed a love for God and His people by watching my mother follow the leading of the Holy Spirit in her journey of becoming a pastor and building a church.

I witnessed my mother gracefully trusting God through the death of the love of her life (my step-father Sidney Goldsby), while still desiring to go deeper in the knowledge and beauty of the Lord. At the age of fifty-two she received her Masters and at the age of fifty-five she received her Doctorate. While I was in college, I answered the call to the ministry because I knew the path was paved and I had someone who would take me by the hand.

As a teacher, preacher, playwright and gifted orator she has made the Word of God come alive for so many. This book will take you on a journey through the life and ministry of Dr. Rosie Goldsby. The bible has proven that for those God calls, He predestined and gives them everything to will and do His good pleasure. It is my esteemed pleasure to not only call her my spiritual leader, prayer partner, confidant and very best friend, but my mother.

Minister Candace Pitts

My Confession

HE LIVES
Written by Alfred Ackley

I serve a risen Savior; He is in the world today.
I know that He is living, despite what men may say.
I see His hands of mercy I hear His voice of cheer.
And just the time I need Him, He is always near.
He lives, He lives Christ Jesus lives today.
He walks with me and talks with
me along life's narrow way.
He lives, He lives, salvation to impart.
You ask me how I know He lives?
He lives within my heart.

T HAT WAS THE song I remember hearing the summer day I gave my life to Christ. I was with my neighbor friend and her mother attending Vacation Bible School at a church other than the one I attended with my parents. Several churches in St Louis City were sponsoring VBS. I was only seven and was raised by Christian parents. Being a part of God's family and going to heaven was talked about all the time. What was different about this invitation to Christ is that my parents were not taking me by the hand while I made my commitment. No, they were not there, but I convinced my older sister to take me up to the front. After I got there, I told her she could leave me if she wanted. (My parents had stood with my other siblings when joining church so I was not so sure if I would face consequences when I got home.)

When I got up to the front of the church the preacher asked my name but I was too nervous to tell him. My teacher for the week along with my adult neighbor came up and gave my name, my parents name, and the church I attended. I do not know if this was true when you were growing up but churches wanted to get credit for new converts and baptisms. My parents must have wanted everyone to get credit so New Salem got credit for my confession. I got baptized at West Side (the church where my neighbors belonged) and my membership transferred to our family home church at Second Missionary Baptist Church of Kinloch. This was the first of my experiences with Christ.

In 1965 my father was working on a rental property he owned next door to our house. He became disoriented and his speech was slurred. A couple of my older brothers were around at the time and they assisted him until he could be rushed to the hospital. My father was around forty and worked a job every day supporting nine kids and a wife. Things were going to get complicated because my mother was in the hospital after delivering child number ten who was born with medical issues and my mother had issues of her own. My oldest sister was about eighteen and child number nine was only about a year old.

An aunt was called and she gave each of us instructions on how to manage the house and keep things going. My father was taken to the same hospital as my mother so she would have the opportunity to visit.

My mother was told my father needed a brain operation and to us that sounded like a death sentence. It must have sounded like that to my aunt because she went to the funeral home and decided to put money down on a funeral for my dad. Although not well herself, my mother got out of the hospital to manage the household. Our younger sister lay in the hospital with a hole in her back (What now may be called Spina bifida).

My father had five brain operations, (3 major and 2 minor, that is the way he always said it.) My baby sister died, my father was still recuperating and money was short. We never missed a meal. Our clothes often came from the Goodwill or Veteran's Village but after my mother washed and ironed them, they looked new.

Out of this tumultuous experience God spoke to my father's heart and he accepted the call to the ministry. In 1966 our small home soon became church on Sunday's and Bible Study on Wednesday. On Saturday nights the living room was converted into the audience seating area with folding chairs and the dining room was converted to the pulpit area and choir stand. Thank God this only lasted a couple of years before the church was built. My father loved the writings of the Apostle Paul and often said, **"I'm a fool for Christ."**

Eunuch Yes/No?

GIRLS USUALLY HAVE their periods by age thirteen and I still did not have mine and I was almost fourteen. I overheard my mother talking to her sister about my delay. They seemed very concerned and I heard my mother say she may have to tell me I will never be able to have children. It took her a while to tell me but one day when she asked me how many children I wanted. I told her I did not want any. It seemed like she breathed a sigh of relief but she knew she still needed to talk to me.

"Our talk" was on the steps of my fathers' church (St John Missionary Baptist Church). My mother had her bible turned to Acts 8:26-40 (KJV). The story is about an Ethiopian eunuch who was reading the book of Isaiah in a chariot owned by Queen Candace when Phillip comes and gives meaning to the scripture. In those few verses the word "eunuch" was mentioned six times but the name of the eunuch was never mentioned. My mother asked me if I knew what a eunuch was and I did not. She told me in this case it was a person dedicated to serve the queen but he could have been "fixed" or born unable to impregnate the women in the queen's court.

I figured this had something to do with me. I was not a man and I did not need to be baptized since I had been baptized for six years. She finally blurted out that I was a "eunuch for THE LORD". I would never have children or get married and my life would be dedicated to the work of the Lord. She told me not to tell anyone and to let the Lord little by little unfold His will for my life. If Mary the mother of Jesus could dedicate her life as a mother and child bride, I guess I could be an instrument for the Lord.

Even though I once played with dolls and pretended to have a husband, the news did not bother me that I would not have a family. I also lived in a small house with ten other family members and growing up and living by myself did not seem too bad. I kept our secret but I started saying that I never wanted to marry or have children. Nobody ever asked me why, so I never had to tell them.

Shortly after I turned fourteen, I was having a lot of monthly stomach pains. Several times my mother let me stay home and one time I heard my mother tell her sister I might be getting ready to come on my period. If I started my period, would I not be dedicated to the Lord?

One day I went to the bathroom and I noticed blood in my underwear. Every time I wiped the blood would keep coming back. I did not know what to do so I just prayed nobody had to use the bathroom before I figured out what to do. One of my sister's was an airline stewardess and she had to come in the bathroom to put on her make-up before she left town.

My sister kept asking me what was taking me so long. Because I did not have an answer, she started pushing me off the toilet. She laughed and said," You started on your period. Here you can use one of my tampons." Before she could tell me how to use it my mother came in. My mother was smart about a lot of things but she knew nothing about tampons and thought we were experimenting with a dildo.

When my sister told my mother about tampons, she seemed to be angry. I did not know if it was because she knew so little about tampons or because she wasn't the first to know that I was no longer a eunuch. My mother told my sister she did not want me to use tampons and she did not think Christian girls should use them. No more conversations were had about eunuchs or tampons.

If not a Eunuch, Then What?

I WANTED TO be dedicated to the service of the Lord so I thought about ways to make it happen. I talked to my friends about Jesus and invited them to church. When they chose to talk in class and misbehave, I wanted to represent Jesus, so I kept quiet. Still, something was missing.

I was reading my bible, attended Sunday School, Baptist Training Union, Bible Study, and anything else that was offered to learn about Jesus. I listened to the sermons but they did not seem to appeal to me until I heard a message preached by my oldest brother John at revival.

I remember the title, "Light Your Own Fire" but not the scripture he referenced. He said if you are struggling with sermons not being to your liking or you are not hearing from God, you need to be more vigilant about seeking the Holy Spirit to come and light a fire in your life. That was what I needed, so right there in the service I started to pray, "God I want you in my life and I want to hear from you. My parents are not telling me the words to say, I'm representing myself." Before I knew it, I felt like the Holy Spirit had entered my body.

I ran from the choir stand and down the aisle to the Pastor's office to call my grandmother. Sometimes when I stayed with her on Sunday night we listened to the service of Lively Stone Church of God and they talked a lot about being filled with the Holy Spirit. She assured me that one day I would receive the Holy Spirit. I was talking so fast she could not understand what I was saying. I kept saying, "I got it, I got it" and told her I would call her back. I could not stay on the phone because I did not want to lose the feeling and I did not want anybody to think something was wrong.

When I went back in the church nobody else seemed to have felt what I felt. First, I was worried that I did not have that "Holy Ghost Fire" my grandmother talked about. Then I heard a voice say, "I'm here." I did not care how anybody else felt because now I knew I was a real representative of the Lord.

Will He Be with Me in College?

I WAS NUMBER seven out of ten children. My mother and father did not complete high school but that was not going to happen to any of their children. I heard my father through the years give my siblings "the speech." "You have three choices when you graduate from high school. You can go to school, get a job, or get out." He believed in "the twenty- two and out of his house program." All of us chose to go to college, at least at the beginning.

Two of my older sisters started college but before finishing they got married. (They each returned and completed later.) My oldest brother started college but was drafted into the army. The next two brothers and a sister all went to the same college, Phillips University in Enid, Oklahoma and completed before getting married. I wanted to go to Baker University in Kansas but my mother forced me to go to Phillips University because my two brothers had graduated from there and my sister would be there by herself. My younger sister and brother also completed college.

Before I could even think about going to college, I had to have a talk with God. I had done well in high school by escaping the traps of physical sins but I was not so sure if I would be so successful in college. Phillips University was a school sponsored by the Disciples of Christ Church. It was not Baptist but it was Christian. My parents liked the school because they had curfew, separate dorms for boys and girls, daily chapel and my siblings maintained good grades during their stay.

When I had my conversation with God I stood in the middle of the floor and it sounded something like this:

> **"God in a few weeks I will be going to college where there is a lot of temptation. I have tried to follow your laws about sexual contact, drinking, drugs, and personal integrity but now I am scared that I might yield to temptation. God, I heard and know you forgive sins but you must know**

that some sins I might enjoy and come back to apologize on a daily or weekly basis. What am I going to do God? If I am going to disappoint you so much that I would not be heaven bound, could you make me a robot? Seriously, do it right now!"

I waited and nothing happened. If you are saying she could not be that naïve, then you are wrong. I loved God so much that I would rather be a robot than to not be in His good graces. Every day I waited for God to answer and when he did not answer by August of 1975, I had to assume that he would love me through the process.

I remember telling my mother that I had some anxiety about going to college and being faithful to God. She told me to get the hymnal out of the piano stool and choose three songs I thought would remind me of my commitment and help during the time of need. The songs I chose were: It Is Well with My Soul, Because He Lives and Blessed Assurance.

I did not tell my parents that I had made up my mind that I would not be going to church while in college and my father did not tell me about his plan to keep me connected to the church. My father had a friend who was a Pastor in Enid, Oklahoma (near the college) and my father told him I would be glad to help as a youth Sunday School teacher and sing in the choir (those were the things I did at my father's church). After missing a couple of Sundays, Rev. Phillips called and said, "Rosa (Rosie) I haven't seen you at church." I told him I was taking some time off but I would be visiting soon. He went on to tell me what he and my father discussed and asked if he needed to call my father. I knew my hands were tied. I told him I would be there next week.

Because I switched schools (from Baker to Phillips) before I could apply for financial aid, I did not get a scholarship. I acquired loans, worked forty hours, and took more than a full course load every semester. I stayed so busy with work, school, and church that I did not have much time to get in trouble. Parties were few and if I did attend, I was there by 8:30 and out by 10:00. I learned on my twenty first birthday that I could not hold my liquor. That was the last time I had a drink.

I did not have to be turned into a robot and I felt God's presence the whole time I was in school. The Holy Spirit warned me of trouble, helped me find inexpensive housing off campus and gave me the stamina I needed to maintain my hectic schedule. I finished my degree in three and a half years and one week after I completed school I was married.

My First Marriage

Obedience is better than sacrifice

I DID NOT have a boyfriend in high school and did not know much about dating. I heard girls should be engaged by the time they get out of college and I had dated only one person in college. I was not going home to my parents so I did the next best thing even though I knew it was not going to work. I decided to marry a divorced man that wanted to live a life that was different than what I wanted to live. We were unequally yoked but I thought I could change him to be the man I wanted. My first husband told me from the beginning I was not his type but he remained in my personal space and I got drawn in.

As I said, the Holy Spirit and I had a good relationship most of the time but sometimes I did not always listen. One case of that was when I married for the first time. On more than one time the Holy Spirit told me the man I was about to marry was not the one God planned for me. I wanted to agree but I wanted to go home, work for Southwestern Bell and live on my own in an apartment. My father did not believe in his daughters living on their own so that meant I would have to go back home and live with my parents and that was not a viable option for me.

A few months before I graduated college my parents met my soon to be husband. My father did not drink, smoke, play cards and always was a sanctified minister. It did not go well when the man I was dating and told my parents I might marry came to night service wearing shorts and with alcohol on his breath. He had just got off the road coming from Oklahoma and in his own way thought he was making a good impression by coming to church.

Towards the end of service my father thought he had a repentant sinner coming to Christ. My father asked him if he wanted to come to Christ. He replied that he was in St. Louis to see his girlfriend Rosie but my father did not think it was "his daughter" Rosie he was talking about. My father gazed over my way and I acknowledged I was the one to whom he referred. I thought my father was going to pass out. This was the first time he ever dismissed church so fast.

When we got out of church we went to my parents' home and my father in no uncertain terms said there was no way he was going to allow us to marry. What my father did not know was my boyfriend at the time was just as stubborn as him.

My first husband was a Sargent in the Airforce and worked in the Communications Department and was strategic in making sure my father did not win. My fiancé knew I never had another boyfriend so he chose to work on the emotions of my heart. My father hoped with enough prayer and guilt, I would change my mind.

My parents refused to help with the wedding so I borrowed a dress from my cousin, made toilet paper flowers (toilet paper came in several colors at that time) to decorate the church. A brother and his wife bought the cake and I bought invitations, peanuts, mints and made punch. My mother gave me the family address book but did not believe I would go through with the wedding. She constantly reminded me that she would really be embarrassed if I went through with it since her friends had come to 6 weddings that were nice.

The men wore maroon tux and the ladies wore pink gowns made by my cousin and sisters. My father allowed me to use the church but as he and I were walking down the aisle he was begging me to turn around and run. The church was filled with people and my sisters were standing up front serving as bridesmaids with tears in their eyes. My brother who was to officiate the wedding was crying as well. As my mother expected, the neighbors were displeased with the reception.

My brother Vernon and his wife Norma let us use their home for our honeymoon cottage since they were going out of town for the Christmas holiday. It was not really needed since my husband told me that night, he only married me because my father said he could not. He said he hated me and had been unfaithful the whole time we were dating. He also shared that he was also having an affair with the married lady that would be living next door to us in Oklahoma.

I could not tell my parents they were right so I just went on to Oklahoma and pretended to be happy. I tried telling my mother things were not so good and she suggested I get pregnant. She said my husband told her he wanted a child. Three months after marrying I was pregnant with a little girl. When she arrived, she was beautiful at 8 pounds 4 ounces. Only a special name would fit her so I named her Candace Elaine meaning, "light from heaven". My husband got out of the military when I was six months pregnant with my daughter and we moved back to Kinloch. Five years later I had a son Paul Anthony, a "small priceless, praiseworthy gift" weighing in at nine pounds.

For five years I felt like I was in prison. My husband constantly called me fat and if I tried to lose weight, he called me names and insisted I was having an affair. To please him I wore dark colors, no make-up and stayed to myself. I lied to my family and only had them over when he was not home.

I spent a lot of time praying through this relationship. My mother told me I was not to consider a divorce because it would embarrass her and God did not agree with divorce. My father did not say anything about divorce good or bad because his mother divorced his father and he loved his mother who was also a minister. My paternal grandmother never remarried and dedicated herself to praying and sharing the plan of salvation with others.

I talked with God daily and I knew he was going to make me remember my disobedience. Every time I went through abuse, I told God I learned my lesson. Several times I threatened to leave the relationship but the Spirit told me to stay and make sure I washed my husbands' clothes, made enough dinner for him even if he did not come home to eat it and never talk to the children (my son was born one month before we permanently separated but the Spirit used the word children) negatively about their father. For five years I struggled to see the value in living with someone who spent more time with his girlfriends and only come home to drop off dirty clothes, pick up clean clothes and make threats.

My husband had many affairs and some of them were out in the open. Whenever I confronted him, his words were, "What are you going to do, divorce me and cause your parents to disown you?" Somebody helped him find scriptures to control me along with abuse.

> **"Likewise, wives be subject to your own husbands, so that even if some do not obey the word, they may be won without a word by the conduct of their wives, when they see your respectful**

and pure conduct. But let your adorning be the hidden person of the heart with the imperishable beauty of a gentle and quiet spirit, which in God's sight is very precious. For this is how the holy women who hope in God used to adorn themselves, by submitting to their own husbands, as Sarah obeyed Abraham calling him lord. And you are her children, if you do good and do not fear anything that is frightening." (1Peter 3 1-6 ESV)

Here is the other one he liked.

"If any woman has a husband who is an unbeliever and he consents to live with her, she should not divorce him. For the unbelieving husband is made holy because of his wife, and the unbelieving wife is made holy because of her husband. Otherwise, your children would be unclean, but as it is, they are holy." (1Corinthians 7:13-14 ESV)

When asked about divorce, Jesus said, "I tell you that anyone divorces his wife, except for sexual immorality, makes her the victim of adultery" (Mark 10:11). I took this statement as the reason I could get out of my marriage. The Lord knew my husband could not keep up his pants.

It took a couple of years for me to realize that in some cases Paul was giving instruction to a particular church about things that were happening in their church community and was not sanctioned for all churches. Paul sometimes gave his opinion and not the Lord's command that had me in a form of prison. I will never believe that God meant for women to suffer in silence and be abused but I do believe God will sometimes leave us in a situation so that we can acknowledge our ways.

Before reading 1Corinthians 7:13-14, I should have read verse 12 and found out that what was being said was Paul's opinion. Even the scripture about a woman not cutting her hair that many husbands declared was the word of God, was again Paul's opinion.

1Corinthians 11:16 says, "If anyone is inclined to be contentious, we have no such practice, nor do the churches of God." Paul shared with the church at Corinth what were some traditions or customs passed along but I believe he was saying that he nor God was holding anyone to them if they loved God with heart, soul, and mind.

I prayed long and hard before I filed for divorce because I know God respects the institution of marriage and it symbolizes the relationship between God and man and the growth of families and the church. Through marriage God shows His 1Corinthians 13th love and reminds us that his love for us is experienced through long suffering.

One evening I remember feeding the kids and going in my room and laying prostrate on the floor. Three hours later the sun had gone down, the kids had fallen asleep and I felt completely wiped out. My prayers were filled with regret that I married a man just to get away from my parents. I prayed that God would forgive me for allowing my husband to marry me even if my husband had his own motives.

I got up off the floor and called my pastor who was my father and asked that he come over. He and my mother came over but I could not tell them anything more than what I experienced; a long time in prayer. My father asked what I had been praying for and I got afraid to tell him because my mother was there. My mother was more adamant about not getting a divorce than my father. She grew up in the "holiness" church and divorce according to her was a sin that could get you to the gates of hell. Not only that, if divorce started in the family, it could become contagious to all my other sisters and brothers who could have been struggling in their marriage.

I just told my parents I needed them to pray for me because I was stressed out and had a lot of bills. My husband was staying with his girlfriend four days a week and came home three days a week to get clean clothes and make sure another man had not come in "his house." My parents prayed and left, but I knew what I had to do if I was going to stay sane.

I found a lawyer but it took me a couple of years to really file for divorce. There was so much to consider.

It is never cut and dry. I had to ask myself if I could accept being called a divorcee, lose my married friends, if I could stand the family pressure, if my kids would think it is all my fault and could I continue paying all the bills. I had not received any support for almost two years and I had learned to pinch every penny twice.

There was a selfish spiritual component to all this madness. When my husband first started spending nights away from home, I wanted to get divorced right away but in my own crazy way I loved him enough to want to see him change so I could take part of the credit for him becoming a man of God.

The Bus Stop

AFTER FIVE YEARS of marriage, I started having dreams of waiting at a bus stop that was at the end of the street where I grew up. I always assumed I was trying to catch a bus to work. Several times the driver would go pass me even though he saw me standing at the bus stop. One day the bus driver opened the door and told me to show my fare and I had a dollar in my hand. He told me to come back when I had exact change. At that time fare was twenty-five cents and for some reason I was hard pressed in every dream to find a quarter. People inside the bus would tell me I was wasting their time and every time I told the bus driver to just keep the change, he told me "No!" and closed the door.

I could not imagine what God was trying to show me. After about four months of dreaming the same dream, I finally had a quarter. The bus came and the driver let me on and everybody clapped for me. I was confused but I hurried and found a seat. When the bus driver finally told me it was my stop and I should get off, I asked him where was I and he said, "You're on the path to new life."

I talked with my father and told him I was going to be getting a divorce and he told me he was happy because he was tired of the abuse. He told me if I ever told my mother he would deny it. I had gone to the lawyer three times and changed my mind so my father gave me sixty dollars and told me when I was serious, come to church wearing a gold dress and then he would believe me. The next Sunday I walked in church with a bronze gold dress and my father was so excited that when he preached, he found himself on top of the pulpit and the deacons had to help him down. That had never happened before and at the end of service we just looked at each other knowing that the biggest part of the challenge was just starting.

I am not happy with what came next. The following Sunday after wearing the gold dress I came to church and my father told me after church come to his house for dinner. I think my father was trying to read my mind and could feel all the confusion I was going through. I told him I would not make any promises. I sat in church but I cannot tell you anything that was said. All I knew was, no sooner than the benediction was given I was out of there.

I made chicken, rice, and green beans for dinner. I fixed my daughter and my plate, and my husband walked through the door after being gone for four days and asked if I saved food for him. I did not answer and he picked up my plate and threw it at me. The hot food went all over my one-month-old child I was holding in my hands. My son was crying and rice was in his face and head. My husband took the phone off the kitchen wall, threw it, laughed, and went downstairs.

As I wiped off the food from my son's face and hands, a killing anger engulfed me. I called my younger brother and asked him if he really meant that he would take care of my children if anything happened to me. He said yes and tried to engage me in conversation but I hung up the phone. I called my husband and asked him to come upstairs. As soon as he stepped into the kitchen, I threw a knife that landed in the wall slightly above his head. I told him I was going to kill him. He laughed again and went downstairs. I decided to use one of the other phones to call the police. I told them I was getting ready to kill my husband and hung up. I did not give my name or number but later they came to the house.

I called my husband upstairs one more time and threw the knife again. This time he believed how angry I was and tried to run out the front door. As he opened the door he ran into the arms of the police and immediately tried to convince them that I was crazy.

With knife in hand, they tried to get me to give it to them but I refused. I told them if they allowed him to stay, one of us would die.

My younger brother showed up shortly after the police and they told him he would have to leave. I remember telling my brother that the kids and I were fine and he could just wait around the corner at our sisters' house. The police asked a lot of questions and finally told my husband he would have to leave the house and they would give him a couple of hours the next day to remove his things.

God was helping me through the whole situation. My brother said when I called him to secure my children's safety, he felt he should get to my house right away because he thought I was having a breakdown. When I called 911 one of my co-workers was also going through police training and answered the phone. He recognized my voice and could not believe I wanted to hurt anyone so he sent the police to my house.

A week after this incident before going to work, an employee from the water company was getting ready to shut my water off. He told me my account was six months behind but he probably could give me until 5pm to pay my bill. I thanked him and decided I needed to check all the utilities and my house payment and they were all six months behind. When we were married, my husband took care of the house note and utilities and I was responsible for paying for his new car, insurance, and groceries. I still wanted to believe he would do the right thing.

God showed me so much favor through the process. My husband took all the money out of the joint account but in less than six months I paid up what was behind along with the current bills. I really should not say I paid them off because it was a supernatural act of God. Every month money was in my account and I have no idea how it got there. The bank said they had no explanation for the money being there and as soon as everything was paid off the money stopped coming. I asked my family members if they had been generous and they had not. None of my friends at the time had that much extra money so I give credit to God. My ex-husband did not know where I banked and I am positive he did not do it. It took two years before our divorce was complete so I supported my children and I on my small salary.

I think about this incident often and thank God for saving me from what my anger could have caused. I thank God that I did not kill my husband and spend time in prison. I thank God I was not losing my mind and that my children would have me to raise them. I thank God that I now could finally be on the "Path to New Life." I did not know what the path would look like but I was sure it would be better than what I had gone through before.

The Call To Ministry

I TOLD GOD I did not want to be a minister. Why cannot I just sing in the choir, teach Sunday School, be the leader for Vacation Bible School and serve as Dean of Christian Education.

Take Time to Be Holy
(Song written by William Longstaff
and George Stebbins)

Take time to be holy. Speak often with the Lord,
Abide in Him always and feed on His Word.

Make friends of God's children.
Help those who are weak,
Forgetting in nothing His blessings to seek.
Take time to be holy, The world rushes on.
Spend much time in secret with Jesus alone
By looking to Jesus, Like Him thou shalt be
Thy friend in thy conduct His likeness shall see.
Take time to be holy. Let Him be thy guide,
And run not before Him, whatever be tide.
In joy and in sorrow, still follow the Lord
And looking to Jesus, Still trust in His Word.
Take time to be holy, be calm in thy soul.
Each thought and each motive beneath his control.
Thus, led by His Spirit to fountains of love,
Thou soon shalt be fitted for service above.

When I was about fifteen one of the missionaries in the church told me she believed God would be using me in the ministry. I did not know what she meant since the National Baptist churches were not accepting of women ministers and neither was my father.

In the early part of my father's ministry, we did not have female "ministers" but women who were called "Missionaries." They were able to speak for Mother's Day and Women's Day and taught Sunday School. I had two brothers who were ministers and a sister who was a missionary but I was not so sure if I wanted a part of that.

There was also Missionary Emma Lee Green, a very intelligent woman who enjoyed serving God and wanted all the children to be smart. She loved giving gifts to encourage us but I did not understand why most of my gifts including for my birthday, were religious books. My sisters and brothers got clothing, shoes, or things they really wanted, but not me.

I really enjoyed reading and I must admit I wanted to know as much as I could about Jesus, but I told my mother if Missionary Green gave me another bible or book for my eighteenth birthday, I was going to tell her I did not want it. Of course, my mother reprimanded me, but I did talk to Missionary Green before I turned eighteen and asked her if she could take me to Famous Barr to get me a pair of leather boots. We went and I was excited because my parents never bought from Famous Barr and I had big legs and never had a pair of boots. Those boots were the best gift I ever had.

By the time I was twenty-two I had a full library of religious materials and two professional Webster dictionaries. I knew to, "Study to show myself approved before God, a workman that need not be ashamed, rightly handling the word of truth. (2Timothy 2:15). I liked my relationship with God even though sometimes I acted like the average young person.

In my twenties I was active in the church. I was in the choir, worked with the young people and was known as the Vacation Bible School lady. I worked for St. Louis County Government helping people find employment. One day while at work a lady who often visited my father's church came by and I thought she was looking for employment. She said she came to deliver a word from the Lord to me. She said while she was in prayer the Lord told her I was going to be a minister. I told her maybe she confused me with one of my sisters since they served as missionaries in the church. She said it was me and I needed to answer the call of God. I nicely told her this was not the place to discuss this and thanked her and told her I had to start work.

A week later the lady came back on a day when I was running a little late for work. When she saw me, she told me she had a word for me from the Lord. I was trying to discreetly tell her she had to leave but she kept getting louder. She said God told her in her kitchen that I was going to preach. I told her God knows I have a kitchen also and if He wants to tell me to preach, He will have to come to my kitchen. From her four-foot frame she wanted me to bend down and let her pray for me. By now several co-workers were around and I walked away and went to my office.

If you ignore God, he will call you out! I knew God was talking to me but I thought it was between He and I. I do not recall it being in my kitchen but I heard the Spirit tell me God needed me to serve. I felt like I was already doing all I could helping people find employment, serving in the church and raising two children. One relative told me I was going to hell since I got a divorce, so in my mind I had ruled out God calling me as a minister.

I started praying more often and listening to the Spirit and I felt the Spirit tell me I needed to be married. I was not going to tell my friends or family that since

I had no idea to whom I would marry. In fact, I did not think I wanted to ever marry again. My younger brother called one evening and said he had just attended a play at University City High School and met one of his girlfriend's co-workers who was looking to re-marry and asked if he could give him my number. I told him I was not running a lonely hearts' club. My brother ignored me and gave him my number.

Sidney Flint Goldsby was a recent divorcee with two boys and a car with no heat. He had joint custody of his sons and told me right away that his priority was to make sure his sons were safe, happy, and loved. I said I wanted the same for my kids. Our first date did not go too well so for our second date I wrote out a list of requirements I expected from a husband. I did not know Sidney had prepared a list also.

Once Sidney made up his mind to marry me, he called and asked for my father's number. I told him I did not think he needed to talk with my father because I was grown. He told me that he wanted to assure my father that he could be trusted to love and protect his daughter and grandchildren. I did not give him the number so he looked in the phone book and retrieved the number. He said the meeting went very well and my father gave his blessings. In just four months after meeting, on May 6,1988 we were married. Sidney was all that I could ask for from a husband and I did all I could to be a good wife.

Seven months after marrying, God decided to show me that he speaks and can get my attention. I loved spicy food and lots of popcorn and it got me in trouble. I went to the doctor and he told me my gall bladder was inflamed and I needed to get it out as soon as possible. I told the doctor I could not do surgery at the present time because I had recently gotten married and did not want surgery the first year. He told me one day my body would decide when the best time would be.

Tuesday December 6, 1988 my body confirmed what the doctor said. While at work the pain was bearable but when I got home it ramped up. By night fall I was hurting so bad I was crying. As Sidney and I laid in bed he would lay his hands on my stomach and pray and the minute he turned over to go to sleep, the pain would come back with a vengeance. I realized I was not getting better and now had a fever. I told Sidney we had to get out of the house immediately because I felt I was not going to make it. He went to the bedrooms to gather the kids and we dropped them off to my brother Milton's house and went to the hospital.

I was in bad shape and the doctor told me that he would need to put me in a comatose state until they could operate. Monday December 12, 1988, they woke me up and told me they were going to operate. I woke up with two feet less of my intestines and the prognosis being fair. I asked God if I was going to die and He said no, He just wanted me to know I did not own time. The voice I heard was not scary or mean just direct and to the point.

The first time I spoke to God, I agreed He owned time and I appreciated Him for all He had done. I pretended to act as if I could not always feel the tug on my heart to totally surrender. In my own way I wanted to convince Him that I was already doing more than most. I was working in my father's church in several capacities, he already had 2 of my brothers as ministers and now 2 of my sisters as missionaries and that was more than most families. God then spoke more definitively and said, "I own time!"

I had Sidney to bring my bible to the hospital and thought I would just go through the bible picking out scriptures that would make me feel better, but that was not God's plan. God said encourage yourself by the scripture you have memorized. At first, I thought I was up for the challenge but after an hour (between breaks), I was speechless. God then told me there is only one verse I want you to keep saying, "In the beginning God created the heavens and the earth (Genesis 1:1 ESV), and if I wanted to go further, read chapters one through four.

My mother and father always went everywhere together but I do not know how my father managed to come alone several days a week to braid my hair. He never said a lot and neither did he stay long after he braided my hair. I think it was just his way of saying he cared.

On Saturday December 17th the doctor told me my insurance company requested I go home and allow them to send a visiting nurse to come in on Monday. I told the doctor I felt I was not well enough to go home but I would try it. I told my husband I wanted to go to my parents' house to spend the night. I could not get comfortable and could tell I was getting worse. My husband called the hospital and they said my insurance company requested that I not come back to the hospital for twenty-four hours.

On Sunday, December 18th I told my parents and husband I would be okay while they went to church, since the church was next door. Once church was over, one of the mothers of the church (Mother's Board) came over to pray for me. She looked at me and said, "Death is in the room." And she laid her body on top of mine and began to pray. After she prayed, she told my father to get me to the hospital right away. When we got to the hospital one of the doctors asked my husband why he waited so late to come back? It was no use telling him what he was told the day before by hospital personnel.

The doctor told me I was going to be in the hospital during Christmas and I was not very happy. On Christmas Eve I heard a Santa coming down the hall saying "HO, HO, HO" and giving people candy. I heard the laughter but I was getting sad because no one could be a better Santa than my mother. (Yes, you read that right.) Every year my mother dressed in her Santa suit and gave gifts and candy to her grandchildren on Christmas Eve. As the sound got closer to my room, Santa sounded more like my mother, and it was. "What do you want for Christmas little girl, she said." I told her I wanted to get out of the hospital but I want to be well. She told me that she and God were still working on that. She gave me a big hug and kiss, gave me a peppermint stick before she left.

I prayed more than ever for God to get me out of there and finally it happened. While sleeping I heard, "You'll be leaving the hospital on New Year's Eve." I told everybody that came in my room that I was leaving on New Year's Eve. I even told the doctor. The doctor told me he could not guarantee that report and he was coming to tell me I needed five pints of blood. I did not get discouraged I just called my brother Vernon and he corralled all my donors up and I got the blood I needed. (He even convinced his secretary to give).

I still had drainage lines and my reports were not good but I believed what I heard. The next time I heard the voice it said I would be healed at 12:00 pm on New Year's Eve. The doctor arranged testing for that day and as I was coming back to my room, I asked the transporter for the time and he said it was 11:55. I asked him if he could not go into the room until twelve but he said he had other patients he had to transport. I told him I could not go in before twelve because God was going to heal me at twelve as I went through the door. He smiled and begin to push me in and I put my hands on the door jams and began to push in the other direction. He realized I really believed what I thought so he agreed to wait the few extra minutes. I did not know my father was inside the room but exactly at twelve my father started saying, "Thank you Jesus!" He told me the church was also praying and at noon they were to say, "Thank you Jesus!"

I informed the nurses to call the doctor because I was leaving. The doctor came a couple of hours later and told me my tests did not come out exactly like he wanted. I told him sometimes God heals immediately and sometimes as we go and I was going home. He was unhappy about my decision but he said if I would be willing to come to the hospital every day for two weeks to get my blood checked and for testing, he would let me go home. I agreed. Within two weeks all drain bags were off and I was much better.

My mother dressed up as Santa and came to visit me in the hospital in 1988 when I had to stay after gall bladder surgery.

A Family That Prays

Dear God,
You chose me as a minister of your gospel. I struggled with my calling because I saw the time it took away from the family, when you called my father into the ministry. We had the fun dad that played horse shoes and cheered for the kids when they were playing ball. We went to the zoo and had picnics in the park. He was not afraid to laugh with or at us and did not call it foolishness. When you commissioned my father to spread the gospel, he no longer had time for us and did not laugh. God I also know that my children will be misunderstood because they cannot hear what I hear or understand the depth of my assignment. Lord, give me fun memories with my children.

SIDNEY AND I had a great marriage considering our blended family. We took time to have date night and tried not ever go to bed angry. I always put notes in his lunch bag and he always brought flowers on Fridays. We took time with the children and they knew that Sidney and I worked as a team and there was not going to be any dissension between us.

Our family loved vacations every year and we called it "Bountiful Blessings." Each year we found one person to which we gave a gift. Sidney and I also gave each of the kids one hundred dollars to buy their siblings a small gift and with the rest of their money they were responsible for buying their snacks while we were away. They used most of the money on themselves but at least they understood the concept of giving and being responsible with money.

We prayed and challenged our children to do what was right even though others did wrong. They did not always get it right but they always had a repented spirit. One of my sons enjoyed reading the bible with me. I always knew if he asked to read the bible with me when the others were sleeping, he was in trouble or was going to get in trouble. After we read, we prayed and I am sure he was asking God for leniency to face his consequences later.

My husband had my sons treat their sister like his princess. They did not like it, and when they could annoy her, they did. She was like the mama when I was not at home and like my assistant when I was.

When she was younger, she loved to sing although her true singing voice did not come to fruition until about fourteen. My husband kept telling her she sounded beautiful and no one should discourage her.

Within the first year of our marriage, I knew God was calling me into ministry and I shared it with Sidney. He was excited and said he supported it and every night he ended by saying, "Good night, Rev." I shared with him what I believed would be God's plans for me and what I needed to do in order to show obedience to Him.

I was use to praying and fasting but this time it was different. Sometimes I would have to pray and fast only eating certain hours of the day. God requested I stop wearing pants while I was praying and at first it was easy. It got harder during the day when people called and asked for prayer or if I was out and people asked me if I would pray for them. God finally told me to get out of pants and now I had to answer questions. Are you saying wearing pants is a sin? Are you going to let your daughter wear pants? Do you think we are sinners if we wear pants? Are you trying to be Pentecostal? Are you sure you heard that right?

I shared with those who asked if wearing pants was a sin, that God never told me that wearing pants was a sin, He just wanted to know if I would be obedient when asked to follow instructions. Because I felt like wearing pants was not a sin, I need not withhold pants from my daughter. At one time the Pentecostal church preached the abstinence of pants for women as a part of the "holiness movement." I was not signifying I was a part of the movement but merely being obedient. I did not wear pants for twenty – two years rain or shine, sleet, or snow. God has told me I could now wear pants. I still choose not to wear pants in church during worship.

As God continued to prune me, I knew I needed a place in my home where I felt like I could feel and hear from the Lord. I bought what I called my prayer stool and placed it next to my bed. Through the years it has been on that stool that I have laughed, cried, and received a Word from the Lord.

God Provides Testing

AFTER SEVEN YEARS of being undercover it was now time to be exposed. I told my husband my father would not be happy with the title "Minister," even though his mother and one of his sisters were ordained ministers. At one point in my fathers' church, women Pastors from other churches had spoken from the pulpit, but now it is a no.

Sidney went to speak to my father and my father tried not to be upset. He told my husband that he being the head of his household should be the one to tell me that I could not be a minister and accept the title of missionary. So as my husband entered the house that day, he announced "I am the head of this household!" Because his demeanor and words were so out of character I started laughing. He repeated the words several times and I laughed harder each time he said it. I did not realize that his vanilla skin was now turning red. It was his son Daniel that said, "Mama, stop laughing daddy is mad."

I stopped laughing but was confused as to why he could be so angry. Sidney announced that when he came from downstairs he wanted to talk to the family.

I grabbed the kids and told them we needed to pray for Sidney. Heads bowed I prayed and then heard a voice say, "Stop praying! I will tell you when this family will pray."

I knew then something major had gone wrong with my loving, spiritually led, family- oriented husband and if this was not contained our family was doomed.

My husband summoned all of us to the kitchen table to sit and be quiet while he tells us how the family would be run from now on. The rules were: 1. We would start having family prayer and he would pray. 2. If we had any questions about scripture come to him. 3. He should be aware of anything happening in our lives and he will be the one to handle any concerns.

I was waiting for my husband to laugh and when he did not, I told him I wanted to speak to him in the bedroom. He got up and led the way. When the door was shut, I asked what was wrong. He laid across the bed and for an hour and said nothing. Finally, he said he had a meeting with Pastor Mitchell to share with him about my calling and the title I had chosen and he would not have any women ministers in the church.

I shared with my husband that for over seven years he had been privy to my calling and preparation and unless God decided to make the change, I am going with what I heard. Sidney said my father was very adamant and said, "I would hate to lose you all as members, but I'm very firm about this son." My husband expressed his desire to stay at St. John and asked if it was possible that I could just not use the title.

Before I could give an answer, one of my sons started knocking at the door to see if I was okay. I confirmed I was and the next question was, "Can we eat?" That made my husband angry and he screamed, "NO! Not until I say so." I told my son to tell Candace to come to the door and when she did, I told her to fix their plates but no seconds until Sidney and I finished talking.

Sidney reminded me that I was not trying to work his new plan. I told him that I married him and not my father and God does not want outside forces to destroy our family. Our family was doing well as a blended family and each of our roles had already been established. We realized this process was not going to be settled in one night so we kissed and held hands as we went into the kitchen to show our united front.

Sidney went to talk to my father again and asked if he could counsel us. My father agreed and told him he thought six sessions on Saturday morning from ten until eleven would give them the desired results. When Sidney brought the idea to me, I hesitated, but because it meant so much to him, I agreed.

At the first conference my father asked me why I thought God called me to be a "missionary." I told him I was not called to be a missionary. I was called to be a minister. He reminded me that three of my sisters (by this time another sister became a missionary) had accepted the title of missionary and he suggested I do the same. I told him I could not because that was not what God told me.

After twenty minutes of my father trying to convince me the title minister was given to men, he decided to take another route and asked me if I respected my husband. I told him I did and that Sidney has been aware of my calling and transition from the beginning. My father looked over at my husband and with a bow of his head he realized this meeting was over and they would need to regroup for the next session.

I knew when I agreed to counseling, I would have to be on top of my game. At the second conference I wanted to share with my father the definitions of evangelist, missionary and minister and none of the titles said anything about gender.

Evangelist – seeks to convert others to Christian faith by public speaking.

Missionary – a person sent on a religious mission.

Minister – a member of the clergy; a body of people ordained for religious duty.

The answer my father gave to all my definitions was that Webster could not address the functions of the church.

The third conference my father did not bother to speak to me, everything was said to my husband. Here are three of the comments my father made. 1.Son, I really thought you had control over your family. If you cannot control your family, how can you get the church members to respect you? 2. Son, this is a new age for women, they think they wear the pants in the house. When she was at home with me, she had no doubt who was the boss. 3. Bro Goldsby, I think you and your wife must decide to leave or stay and when you do, just let me know. Much success to you.

Before I left that third and final session, I told my father that he disrespected my husband more than I ever could. I told him I learned from the best how to handle people who do not want to accept God's will for my life. I told him I remembered after his 5 brain operations that people teased him when he said God called him into the ministry and was going to allow him to build a church. Within two years of my father starting church in his home, a church was built to God at 5409 Case in Kinloch. I told him I loved him and gave him his favorite quote, "I'm a fool for Christ."

Sidney asked several of his male friends what they thought about women in ministry. Some said they did not agree and some went on to say that our marriage will end in divorce. His brother Miles and his friend

Everett said they believed I was called and he should support me. He never stopped being a loving and caring husband and we continued to pray together at night but we did not talk about titles until one night in September 1996.

It Is Time

IN SEPTEMBER OF 1996 the Spirit of God told me it was time for me to stand up and be counted as one of his ministers. I called my younger sister Madeline and my sister Linda to tell them I was going to stand up as a minister not a missionary. They both laughed and said I was going to be put out of church. I told them I had to take that chance.

I was working as a secretary at my father's church and was due to go in. I decided this was the day I needed to resign. I told my father I appreciated serving the church but I had to stand up for what I believe God was calling me to do. He said he no longer needed my service and I could give him the keys. I did, and then left.

I went over to my Uncle Edward's house to complain about his brother but he said he could not help me because he was not sure how he felt either. While we were talking the phone rang and I answered it. It was my Uncle Mel, the brother of my uncle and father. As I was about to hand the phone over to Uncle Edward he said, "I don't want him, I called to talk to you." He told me the Spirit told him to tell me to do as God says even if my father or anybody agreed. I asked him if my father had talked with him and gave information about "my calling." He said the Lord told him about it and told him to call me at my uncle's house. I was stunned because this uncle lived in Chicago.

I did not call my husband at work. I figured I would let him know when he got in. My father did not have a problem calling him. Sidney came home and was not pleased that "we" were leaving the church (I never said "we"). He said "we" were not leaving, and until God gave me some firm plans for my ministry, I should not say anything to anybody about my ministry.

If anybody would understand what I was going through it would be my sister Linda, so I told her I needed to talk to her the next day. My sister Linda was never lackadaisical when it came to doing the will of God. The minute the Holy Spirit gave her an assignment she started on it right away. Once, the Spirit of God told her to reach out to sinners by sharing the Word in the bi-ways and highways. She went to the Christian bookstore, bought leaflets, and stood on corners in neighborhoods and yes on the exits off the highway.

She never asked anyone to help her because she knew people would feel uncomfortable as their friends and family viewed them as they stood next to the homeless and offer a word of hope. I was surprised one day while driving, to see her standing on the corner near the highway passing out leaflets and praying for people. I parked my car, asked her if she was okay and she replied yes. I got back in the car and thanked God for that not being my ministry.

When I spoke with her the next day, she allowed me to express some of my hesitations. I told her I thought if God gave me an assignment, I should have more supporters. She laughed and asked me where did I find that in the bible. She reminded me that we had a nursing home and hospital ministry together but she was not going to go further than that to make me feel better. She prayed for me and left.

The next day while in prayer, I saw myself as a pastor but did not see anyone else helping me. I asked God could he send someone to help me since He always sent his disciples out by twos. No news for a couple of days but I felt my assistant was on the way. Saturday September 28th around 7:30 am my sister Linda came to the house without calling. When I opened the door, she was angry and said, "Why did you tell God to make me help you?" I told her I did not give Him a name but I was glad she was willing. She sneered at me and said, "Put your clothes on we're going to talk to daddy." I told her I could not do that, I had to first talk to my husband. She said if I was scared to talk to him, she would talk to him. Before I could reply she was yelling for my husband to come and meet her in the kitchen for a cup of coffee. I told you when my sister Linda has an assignment from God, there is no room for delay or further instructions.

I dare not go back to the bedroom and give my husband the reason why he was being summoned so I just started making coffee. It was not unusual for Linda and Sid to drink coffee in the morning. When Sidney got in the kitchen, Linda said they needed to go downstairs to his office to talk. My sister came back up first and said Sidney believed God called her but he was not sure about my calling. She said she knew God called us to be ministers but was not going to wait on Sidney's approval. She left my house going to our parents' house to tell them the news.

When Sidney came upstairs, he was not angry just bewildered. He did not say anything as he walked past me and neither did I to him. I got the kids up and gave them breakfast trying to act as if the last hour or so did not happen. I left my husbands' breakfast on the stove. Just as I was leaving out of the kitchen, I looked in the window and saw Linda had returned.

"We do not have a church to go to anymore so we might as well start church tomorrow. I am going home to talk to John to see if we can start having church in our home tomorrow." I told her I was not going to be ready by tomorrow and she said, "You can join in when you get brave enough to stand and do God's work without hesitation." She left.

I went in the bedroom and Sidney was laying across the bed with his arms behind his head. When I walked in, he said, "Well, what are you going to do?" I told him Linda went to talk to my parents representing the both of us and told them we were ministers and if they could not accept it, we were leaving. She was now asking John if she could hold service in the house on tomorrow. I told him I could not imagine John giving her an answer right away and thought we may have a couple of weeks to digest all that was going on.

I asked him if he really believed God did not call me to minister and he said, "I believe God is not the author of confusion." I reminded him of the last couple of years of my spiritual grooming and how he always said, "Good night, Rev." He said he remembered but things were not going as he imagined. He said he was not leaving my father's church even if I did and the kids were going to church with him.

Linda called an hour later and said John gave approval and she was going to start getting the church together. I told her we did not have a name so she said she would write a couple of names down and I should do the same. Before she hung up, she asked me if I was all in and I told her I could tell her more later that evening.

I went in my bedroom and prayed and told God I was not a coward but could he make things right with my husband. The only thing I knew when I finished praying was that I needed to give the kids their Saturday assignments and go to the Christian bookstore to get communion supplies.

About two o'clock Linda tried calling me on my cell phone but the call would not come through. We called each other for almost twenty minutes with no success. When I became totally frustrated, I went to the Church's Chicken Restaurant on Halls Ferry Road and sat on the parking lot. A few minutes later Linda showed up and parked next to me not recognizing I was parked next to her. When I saw her, I got out of my car and then she got out of hers and we hugged as if we had not seen each other for years. We both agreed that we did not know what caused us to come to Church's Chicken.

I told her to get in her car and follow me home. When we got in the house, we sat at the kitchen table and recapped the day. Now it was time to think of the name of the church and denomination. She thought we should be a Baptist but I told her that was part of the group that was unaccepting of women in ministry. I told her let us be Non-Denominational and she agreed. We tossed around all the names we had written down and we agreed on the one that was on her list which was "The Temple." That day we became The Temple Non-Denominational Church,10544 Monarch with services starting Sunday September 29th at 10am.

I gave my husband all the information from the day and gave him as much attention as he thought he could accept. I also told him I had to do what God wanted me to do but I would come and be with he and the kids as soon as our services were over every Sunday.

There were about twelve people attending the first Sunday and Linda took the lead as pastor. Her family were the first members along with several neighbors. Linda preached her first sermon and I did the devotion. A few weeks later a pastor friend of ours agreed to ordain Linda. He organized a panel of ministers to ask questions and Linda was nervous. Every time she was a little slow answering, I nervously said the answer aloud. I kept apologizing saying she studied that question and knew the answer. I am glad they did not throw me out.

For the next three months I attended the Temple and then went to St. John to be with my family. Our kids had questions about what was going on but would not ask my husband. I got questions like: Did grandpa make you mad and you do not want to be around him anymore? Are you going to ever sing in the choir or do Vacation Bible School? Can we go to church sometimes with you? Why can't you just be a minister at St. John? Are you ever coming back to St. John? Are you and dad going to get a divorce? I could not answer any of the questions but I hoped Sidney and I would not get a divorce.

After three months of waiting to see what my husband was going to do, I joined The Temple Non-Denominational Church on January 12, 1997. It was a day of mixed feelings but I knew it was time. I was actively participating at The Temple and the membership was growing. In three months, we bought a portable baptismal pool and baptized several people on my sisters back porch. On February 9, 1997 I was ordained and thought I had overcome my biggest hurdle.

Later that month God asked me a question that I told him I would not answer. He said, "If I take your husband, will you still preach?" I knew from the relationship I had with God that he was not really asking, he was telling me. I knew I had to be careful how I responded because he had already told me "He owned time." I wrestled with that question and could not share it with anyone.

The question became a nightmare that caused me to toss and turn and talk in my sleep. My husband woke me up one night and told me I had been talking in my sleep for a couple of weeks and I needed to explain what was going on. I pretended to act like I did not know what he was talking about but he would not let me off the hook. He asked me if I was being harassed by someone and if I had, he could help me handle it.

I sat up in the bed and told him, God said, "If I took your husband will you still preach." Then I said, "I told Him I wasn't going to answer Him because he was going to take you anyway." Sidney grabbed me by the arm and pulled me to his side of the bed and onto the floor as he positioned himself next to me.

He said he could not believe I would jeopardize our family by not answering God. He reminded me that if something would happen to the both of us our children would not have the same opportunities they have now. He told me we were going to pray and when it was my turn, I better tell God how sorry I was for not answering. When we got up, he grabbed his pillow and the extra blanket and started for the couch in the family room. I was concerned about what it would look like to the kids if we were sleeping separately so he said he would be back in the room by five.

I do not think either of us got any sleep. When he came to the room in the morning, he told me he would be sleeping on the couch for a while. After the third night while he was in the family room, he said aloud, "God, if I am going to be a hindrance to my wife's ministry, please let me know." The sound of thunder was so loud, it shook the house. I ran in the room where he was and asked him why he said that. He said at least now we both knew. There was no inclement weather outside to contribute to what we heard and the kids stayed asleep through it all.

I did not know when God would take my husband but we had several discussions about it. We had discussions about what I should do when he died and what he wished for me. We made sure we spent a lot of time together and on the Sunday's I preached, he always came to hear me and then went to St. John.

My daughter and son became members at The Temple and Sidney's sons remained with him at St. John. At meals my husband started reminding us about our commitment to God and the importance of family love. I do not think he told anyone about that thunderous night but I often prayed that his death would not be soon. Sidney believed God was going to do something and wanted to make sure he worshipped. In church service at St. John, he started doing what the kids called," Jumping for Jesus." Sidney would run the width of the church and just when you thought he was going to run into the wall, he would jump and go back the other way. If the Lord was not with him, I think we would have been in the emergency room a couple of times.

One night he called both of his sisters and asked for forgiveness for things he had done as a kid. When he got off the phone, I asked him why he needed to do that and he said he had to wipe his slate clean. He even called some old friends he had not seen in years and asked for forgiveness for misunderstandings they may have had. They were not sure what he was talking about but was glad to hear from him.

The two hardest conversations he needed to have, was with his brother Miles and his best friend Everett. They supported my ministry from the beginning and told Sidney they were going to tell me so. Sidney had stopped talking to them as much and had stopped going to the gym with his best friend at lunch. He thought if he apologized and allowed his friend to win at chess that would suffice for him but he knew he would have to meet face to face to apologize to his brother and play a little basketball.

Our Long Trip

JULY 3, 1997 we were packed and ready to go to Virginia Beach, Virginia to see Miles and Tracey. Sidney 111 was staying behind to work and Candace was going to Kentucky with her father. So, with our two boys Daniel and Paul, we headed down the highway. We took the scenic route and at the midway point we decided to get a hotel and spend the night.

I knew I wanted Shoney's the next day for breakfast and it did not take much to get the others on board. We got on the road around seven and agreed on a ten thirty stop so we could eat breakfast. Around ten, the Spirit told me I needed to start fasting immediately because someone close to me was sick unto death. I pulled out my phone and called my mother because she had recently gotten out of the hospital. With her usual cheery answer when someone calls, "Hello, may God bless you." I knew it was not her. I asked to speak to my father and he sound fine also.

Because this announcement of concern was standing in the way of my breakfast, I called everybody I considered first line family and friends and everybody said they were fine. When my husband pulled up to the restaurant, he ran around to my door to let me out and I told him he and the boys should go in and eat because I needed to continue fasting and prayer. He asked if he should bring me a "to go" plate and I told him no because I did not know what time I would be allowed to eat. I think Sid made the boys eat fast because they returned to the car in under forty-five minutes. I could not imagine who could be sick enough to die but my father always said, "Your wellest days, you're sick enough to die."

As we got close to Norfolk, Virginia, Sidney asked me if I was still concerned about what the Holy Spirit was saying to me. I told him I was and that I could not imagine who it was. Sid had done quite a few things to distract me along the way by playing bible trivia and allowing me to sing almost fifty songs out of the hymnal I brought. He then decided to give me his personal desires he had for the kids and what he wanted God to do upon his death to let me know he was okay. I wrote down what he wanted each of the kids to know and what he wished for them. He even told me what he wished for me. Lastly, he told me he asked God to allow him to come back as a red bird (preferably a cardinal) and to place a rainbow in the sky. We laughed for a while and then held hands until we got to his brother's house.

It was July 4th and the festivities were at the Johnson's (Tracey's parents) so we quicky unloaded and headed that way. God gave me a one-hour period in which I could eat. We had a great time with Tracey's family and when it was getting dark, we returned to Miles and Tracey's home. Miles, Tracey, Sidney, and I stayed up late talking. Sidney and Miles squashed their disagreement and they challenged each other to a basketball game in the morning. We were planning to stay ten days so it was going to be a lot of "smack talk" over chess, dominoes, and basketball.

On July 5, 1997 at 5:15 am my husband woke me up and said, he had something to talk to me about. I did not know what to think but I sat up in the bed and listened. Sidney told me he wanted me to know that he "always loved me." My heart sank and started beating fast. Before he could say his next sentence, I told him if he was having an affair could he wait until we got back home to tell me. He kissed me and told me he was not having an affair and never thought about having one. He just wanted to assure me that through all we had been going through his love for me had never waned.

He apologized for not always understanding my calling and creating an atmosphere of dissention. He told me the Spirit of God had talked with him and confirmed my calling. He also said two of our children would be called into the ministry. He reaffirmed that God should be first in my life and if he should come back home, he would join The Temple and work with Linda and I.

Because I heard the words, "I always loved you" and "if he should make it back home" I asked him if he was sick and he said no. He said he just wanted to clear the air and assure me that everything was going to be better once we got home.

I suggested that we get up and go walking and spend some time looking at the scenery in Virginia Beach. When we returned to the house around 7:00am Sidney's brother and wife had started fixing breakfast. We ate and sat around talking for a while.

I told Tracey I had seen some signs for garage sales and we should go and check them out. She agreed. We found a lot of great buys and we talked about where we might go to dinner. When we got back home around 11:00 the guys were standing around trying to decide what they were going to do first. Should they go to the community center to play basketball or go to the beach? Sidney was standing against the wall near the front door and as I was passing by, he grabbed my hand and told me, "I'm not ready to go." I turned to the boys and asked them could not they wait until later to go somewhere and they agreed they could. Sid said, "No, we're going to the gym, that's where we're supposed to go." He held me tight and said, "Remember I've always loved you."

Again, I asked him if he was okay and he said, "Yes." He told the boys to get ready to go and as they were coming down the stairs, they told Sid they had something for him. It was a shirt that said, "We're going to beat you so bad in basketball they're going to have to put your name on a school milk carton to find you." We all laughed and could not wait to hear the truth and half-truths of the impending basketball game.

When Sid, Miles, Daniel, and Paul went to the community center to play basketball there were other men that challenged the Goldsby's to a game. One thing you should know about the Goldsby's is they do not back down for anybody when it comes to basketball. One game led to another and after which they also played racquetball. Sidney mentioned he was feeling tired so it was suggested that they get into the pool to relax. While in the pool Sidney said he needed water and got out of the pool. When he bent over to drink, he fell to the floor.

In the meantime, my sister-in-law Tracey and I were at the house and she suggested I sit down and watch a video of her Pastor's sermon while she washed clothes. She put the video in and after she left, I heard a voice say, "You help everybody else, let's see how you handle this." This was not a human voice and I was not so sure why I was being harassed. I yelled, "Just shut up!" Tracey reentered the room and asked what I was saying and why had the video stopped playing. I told her I did not touch the video and I was just thinking out loud. I was not about to tell her I was talking to the devil.

Tracey started the sermon again and went back to her washing. This time the voice said, "This is it! Let us see what you do." Again, I spoke out loud and this time said, "You're a liar!" Tracey came back into the room and again asked why the video was off again. I told her I did not know why the video and television was off. She turned them back on and this time took the remote with her.

I knew something was happening but could this really be the end? Shortly after that incident my son Paul called and said, "Mama, if you want to see Dad you better get here right away because Dad looks like he's dying." I could not understand why he was calling me because he did not have a cell phone and he was with his Uncle Miles and his older brother. I wanted to ask a lot of questions but he kept saying in a frantic voice, "Mama you better get here fast! Go get Aunt Tracey and get over here."

We were only a little over two miles away but it seemed like five. When I walked in the community center Sidney was on the floor and the EMT's were working on him. I got on my knees and told Sidney he better get up because there was no way I could drive the van back through the mountains to St. Louis. I thought if he heard my desperation, he would try harder to come back to us. I jumped up and decided to call my dad, Sid's best friend Everett Jefferson and my younger sister Madeline and told them Sid was very sick and needed prayer.

I ran back in the building hoping to see some improvement but there was none. I bent down again and told Sidney he had to get up, but to me he just gave a quick smile. I got up, and as I stood there, I could feel heat rising. The heat was now pressing against my lips. I closed my eyes for a minute and then told the EMT's he was gone. They said they were going to continue trying until they took him to the hospital. On that three-mile ride in the ambulance to the hospital, I composed myself and tried to think of what to do next. I knew it was over.

Miles, Tracey, and the boys came shortly after us and we sat down waiting for the results. When I saw the doctor coming from around the corner headed my way, I knew what he was going to say. He gave his condolence and I began making a few phone calls. The nurse came back to tell the boys and I we could go back to see Sid. I could not break down, so we sung I will Fly Away and repeated the 23rd Psalm and the boys gave him a hug and kiss.

When we returned to the waiting room some of the guys with which he played basketball were there to give their condolence. Miles also called his pastor and got the name of a funeral home. When we arrived back at Miles house, a deacon and minister came by the house to assist the family. Shortly after they left, the funeral director arrived.

We sat in the family room where the patio door was visible. After talking for over an hour, the funeral director asked me if I knew anything about birds and I asked him why. He said a cardinal had been on the patio ever since he sat down and had been walking back and forth. I told him I had seen him also but he should not be alarmed because it was my husband making sure all the arrangements were done professionally and at the best price. Because I did not laugh and appeared very serious, he asked me if he needed to get my brother-in-law. I told him he did not and I was very aware of what I was saying.

Before we could continue conversing, Miles came running in the house. He informed me that there was a rainbow in the sky above the house and it was not raining. I told him it was the sign that Sidney was okay. We rejoiced and I waved and Miles took the boys to the beach to sail the t-shirt they intended their father to wear after the basketball game.

Saturday night I did not sleep much but I knew I was going to church Sunday morning. Isaiah 61:3 (KJV) reminds us, "For the spirit of heaviness put on the garment of praise" so I needed to get moving and find me a church. I got dressed knocked on Miles and Tracey's bedroom door and told them I was going to find a church to attend. They told me give them a minute to get dressed and we could go to the church they attended because they were celebrating their pastor's anniversary.

By Monday I was headed back home to complete the arrangements for the funeral. Miles and Tracey accompanied me back home by air and Susan and Rozzell drove the boys' home in the van. I was blessed to get so many things done in such a short period of time. I knew family support made it possible.

Sidney's homegoing service was well attended and was Spirit-filled. There were people upstairs, downstairs, and even outside. He worked as a Chemist and Computer Specialist for the Food and Drug Administration and had earlier worked for the Department of Agriculture. Sidney also owned a computer business named Pure Gold that helped churches download and backup data.

No Time To Waste

O N JULY 13TH I was
back in position at
The Temple. Sometimes I felt like I needed to take
off but instead prioritized things so I would not spend
too much time thinking. I realized my financial
circumstances was going to change drastically and the
church was not financially able to give me a salary. My
husband's job would provide some assistance but I did
not know if it was enough to pay all my bills or how fast
I would get it. I checked my account and knew I would
be good for about six months. I had now been a stay-
at-home mom for six years and may have to get a job.

Two months passed by and I started getting nervous.
I called to see how fast I would get assistance from my
husband's job and they said as stated before, the check

most likely would not get to me before six months. I began to worry and pray. I guess God got tired of me fretting so at 2am one night he woke me up and told me to get my bible and turn to Isaiah 54:5-17 (KJV) and claim that as my promise from Him.

5 For thy Maker is thine husband; the LORD of hosts is his name; and thy Redeemer the Holy One of Israel; The God of the whole earth shall he be called.

6 For the LORD hath called thee as a woman forsaken and grieved in spirit, and a wife of youth, when thou wast refused, saith thy God.

7 For a small moment have I forsaken thee; but with great mercies will I gather thee.

8 In a little wrath I hid my face from thee for a moment; but with everlasting kindness will I have mercy on thee, saith the LORD thy Redeemer.

9 For this is as the waters of Noah unto me: for as I have sworn that the waters of Noah should no longer go over the earth; so have I sworn that I would not be wroth with thee, nor rebuke thee.

10 For the mountains shall depart, and the hills be removed; but my kindness shall not depart from thee, neither shall the covenant of my peace be removed, saith the LORD that hath mercy on thee.

¹¹ O thou afflicted, tossed with tempest, and not comforted, behold, I will lay thy stones with fair colors, and lay thy foundations with sapphires.

¹² And I will make thy windows of agates, and thy gates of carbuncles, and all thy borders of pleasant stones.

¹³ And all thy children shall be taught of the LORD; and great shall be the peace of thy children.

¹⁴ In righteousness shalt thou be established: thou shalt be far from oppression; for thou shalt not fear: and from terror; for it shall not come near thee.

¹⁵ Behold, they shall surely gather, but not by me: whosoever shall gather together against thee shall fall for thy sake.

¹⁶ Behold, I have created the smith that blows the coals in the fire, and that bringeth forth an instrument for his work; and I have created the waster to destroy.

¹⁷ No weapon that is formed against thee shall prosper; and every tongue that shall rise against thee in judgment thou shalt condemn. This is the heritage of the servants of the LORD, and their righteousness is of me, saith the LORD.

Before that night, that scripture did not mean a lot to **me.** I knew the text referred to Israel straying from God and He allowing them to be forgiven and brought back to Him, but now it became personal. I got on my prayer stool and recommitted my trust and reliance on God by reminding myself of what Proverbs 3:5-10 (KJV) says, "Trust in the Lord with all your heart and lean not unto thine own understanding. In all your ways acknowledge Him and He will direct your paths. Be not wise in your own eyes: fear the Lord, and depart from evil. It shall be health to thy navel, and marrow to thy bones. Honor the Lord with thy substance, and with the first fruits of all thine increase: so, shall thy barns be filled with plenty, and thy presses shall burst out with new wine."

The Spirit led me to put all my bills in my bible and declare my reliance on God. I slept well the rest of the night and felt refreshed. Doubt could no longer be a part of my day. I went about the day singing and rejoicing because I felt like God was about to do something, and He did. When I went to the mailbox the next day, I received the check I was expecting. I opened it and started rejoicing, but first I needed to make a call. I called my husbands' job to see if the check had been sent and they said it was not. They told me they had not sent anything but they would see what they could do to expedite the check. I told them OKAY but knew God had already given me what I needed and was on my side.

Later that week in dreams, I started seeing a church building in Castle Point, Missouri but to the naked eye there was nothing available. After I asked my sister Linda if God had said anything to her, she said she felt like God was saying it was time to build. We would drive and walk up and down the street searching for a parcel of land that was about an acre or two, but to the naked eye there was no cleared off parcel to be had.

Linda went to Clayton to check for undeveloped land for sale and was made aware of two fifty-foot parcels and she called me to see if it was okay to buy it. I agreed but told her it was not enough to start. She was later told there were over two acres connected to the two parcels but they were owned by thirteen individuals. The average person would give up and call it a day, but Linda saw it as a challenge to see if all thirteen people would give up the land for the work of the Lord.

I have told you about Linda's persistence when she feels God has given her an assignment, so it will not surprise you that Linda got the names, addresses and telephone numbers of each of the land owners and made an appointment for us to talk to them. The first appointment was with a couple who owned the connecting property to the two small parcels we bought. When we entered the house, the man was laying on the couch and the lady led us to the kitchen.

After we sat down Linda started right away telling her, "God had need of something she had," and gave her the address to the property. The lady started screaming and crying, apologized and said she had a dream that her mother was telling her to give the property she formally owned away for her birthday. She did not understand what it meant but now it all made sense. The day we came to see the lady was her mother's birthday. The lady ran to her bedroom and got the papers and signed them over to us. She told us she wanted nothing in return except for us to pray for her husband who had back problems and had not seen his mother or gone to work in six months. She also shared she was having some depression problems and wanted God to take it away because it was affecting her work performance.

Linda and I had already agreed on our assignments for this project and mine was to pray. I asked the lady if she would come in the room with her husband so we could pray for them both. After we prayed, we did not hear from them again until our church was built and she came to the grand opening. It was her testimony that caused the people to praise God. She shared that after we left her house that day, her husband started walking again, went to see his mother and shortly afterward returned to work. She too was healed of her depression and no longer needed medication.

There is a story behind each of the lots that we obtained. Two parcels were given to us after we paid the taxes on them, which was minimal. Two other parcels were bought for less than a thousand dollars and the others were just signed over to us. We now had all the lots but we did not have the money to build. God was about to do something but what?

Earlier I shared with you a scripture from Proverbs 3:5-10 (KJV). Look at verse 9 again. "Honor the Lord with thy substance and with the first fruits of all thine increase."

God made a request for me to give $100,000 (yes one hundred thousand dollars) to help with the building of the church. I must admit that I was not in total agreement at the beginning because I thought I heard wrong. I wrestled with it but He wrestled with me. I told Him I was unemployed, had bills to pay and could not see giving that much. He reminded me of my Isaiah 54 scripture and I finally told him if it was Him telling me to do it, he would have to confirm it through someone else. I put a check with the exact amount in a white envelope.

The next day my younger sister called and said she had a dream about me holding an envelope and asked if I knew what she was referring to. I told her I did, but would tell her later. I called my sister Linda over and gave her the check and told her the Lord was giving the church its first contribution to the building fund. When she opened the envelope, she asked if I could really cover the amount on the check. I told her I could and she started rejoicing.

We still did not have enough money to build a church so that meant we had to go to a bank and ask for some. We went to a couple before we found one that would give us the money. The man at the bank that eventually gave us the money thought it was ridiculous for us to ask for money and the church was only a year old. He first refused to sit with us until my sister told me to start praying for him. The man got nervous and told us he would give us an application and it would take about six months before it would be ready to be presented to the board. He thanked us for coming and hurried to his office.

One week later we were back at the bank with all the papers completed. The banker could not believe we completed the assignment so quickly but my sister and I was not sleeping very much during that time to get everything done. We had to get references, credit checks, lot surveyed, meet with the city hall, and temporary plans for our impending building. God opened doors to every place we needed to go.

The banker reviewed what we had and agreed we had what we needed for our paperwork to be presented to the board but said they would never accept it. Linda asked if he would like her to go and present our request to the board and he quickly said no. She then asked if we could pray for him so that he would be successful with our proposal. Hesitantly he agreed but told us not to say anything that would be harmful to him. That same day he had a scheduled board meeting and presented our proposal, and they agreed to give us the money. (The banker and us became good friends.)

From start to finish of the building project, God was in control. We knew and felt God's power with us and tried our best not to go ahead of Him. Our failures came when we assumed God supported all our thoughts and actions. I could tell you about twenty super natural stories of how God used people to bless the project but that will have to be in the next book.

God allowed our members to have "hands on experience" putting in insulation and doing small projects. They now had ownership and knew the importance of trusting God, paying tithes, and offering and studying the word of God. Linda and I along with Uncle Edward acted as contractors. We worked long hours and believed God for the fruition of the building.

All Things Work Out For The Good

Therefore, my beloved brethren, be steadfast, immovable, always abounding in the work of the Lord, knowing that your labor is not in vain in the Lord. 1Corinthians 15:58 (NKJV)

THE FIRST FIVE years of our ministry my father refused to answer to the name "Daddy" for my sister Linda and I. He told us we should call him "Pastor Mitchell." One day when I called the house, my mother answered the phone and said, "Hello may God bless you" (her usual opening). I said, "Hey mama" and she said, "This is Sister Mitchell." I thought maybe she did not hear me so I said, "Hey mama", and she said, "This is Sister Mitchell."

I had a decision to make. Should I consider this a personal attack or am I calling to see how she is doing? I wanted to see how she was. Knowing the closeness of my parents, it is a good possibility my father was in the room. Each time I called her "Sister Mitchell," I realized she was hurting because in some ways, I was denying her as my mother.

I did not hate my parents and thought of them as my testers. All my life my parents taught us how to stand up for ourselves and be an example for God. This was just my next phase of testing. Out of all the people in the world, these are the people I respected the most and knew they were only making me strong enough to handle the criticism of the world. I do not pretend it did not hurt, because it hurt!

After the church was built, several pastors that were friends of my father stopped by. They song our praises and said a man could not do as much as we did. Each one asked if my father had come by and I told them he had not. The word got out and my father made an appointment to see the church. He inspected the walls, floors, heating, our auditorium, and offices and walked out not saying much other than, "Somebody did a good job." I wanted to hear him say something different but we had more testing to complete.

Our family was big on holidays and my parent's loved visits from their grandchildren. My sister and I swallowed our pride and made sure our kids had visits with them even if it meant we were not welcome. My parents expected my other sisters and brothers to believe as they believed and, in this case, they opted to be quiet about how they felt about our ministry. I knew my younger brother and sister thought we were doing the right thing and often attended morning worship.

My older brother was running a revival at the church he pastored and I decided to attend the service. After devotion he welcomed all visiting ministers to the pulpit. I did not dare move to the front and possibly be embarrassed. I thought about the story when Jesus said, "When you are invited by someone to a wedding feast, do not sit in a place of honor, lest someone more distinguished than you be invited by him, and he who invited you both will come and say to you, "Give your place to this person, and you will begin with shame to take the lowest place." (Luke 14:7-9 ESV)

After all the men were seated, my brother made an announcement. "My sister Minister Rosie Goldsby is in the audience and I would like her to come sit in the pulpit with the rest of us." I thought I was going to pass out. I looked around to make sure no one else was going to go up and then quickly moved before he changed his mind. He went on to say that he supported the ministry of my sister and I and hoped to be visiting us soon.

Shortly after I considered myself comfortable, my father walked in the church. He usually is never late for church but this time he was. Our eyes met when he was coming up the aisle and immediately my brother got up and welcomed him to sit next to him in the pulpit. He also said it was great to have a father and sister in the ministry worshipping with him. I took a couple of deep breaths and enjoyed the service.

I could not wait to call my sister Linda to tell her what happened. She had me to tell her the story a couple of times to make sure I did not leave out anything. We went to the church the next day and looked at our calendar to see when we could have a revival and invite my brother to speak. The date was set and he said he even thought my father would come. Who knows, this could be the end of the great divide. The day came, the sermon preached and at the end when my father was given the opportunity to speak, he thanked my brother for inviting him to the service. He said nothing about my sister and I.

Five years went by before my father realized he could not fight what God was doing with his girls. One of his friends told me he talked to my father and asked him what man did he know that could build a church and have a ministry like ours without the guidance of the Lord. To that I say, "Amen." Shortly after that, my father invited me to his church and had me sit in the pulpit. He stood up gave his text and said he was excited about the message he was going to preach. He then said he was going to preach his sermon next week and told me to get up and preach a sermon for the people. I panicked for a minute but then remembered what he told my brother's about always keeping a sermon in their bible. I thanked God I had just left my church and had my sermon in my bible.

My two sisters who were missionaries became ministers as well. My oldest sister went to another church to serve and my sister that is a year older than me served under my father and later became the pastor of the church he founded.

Brothers and sisters, think of what you were when you were called. Not many of you were wise by human standards, nor many were influential; not many were of noble birth. But God chose the foolish things of the world to shame the strong. (1 Corinthians 1:26-27 NIV)

Acknowledgements

I want to thank my supporters through the years who have encouraged me in some way. Even if your name is not included on this page, know that you are forever in my heart.

To God who gave me an assignment and put people in place to encourage, test and produce the desired outcome.

To Yeshua/Jesus my brother and Savior who set his life priority to do the will of the Father.

To the Holy Spirit who led me into prayer and praise that provided comfort and pushed me into submission.

To my mother and father, Pastor John and Sis. Rosie Mitchell who challenged me to stand firm in the gospel.

To my sisters and brothers who when called out to preach the gospel, accepted.

My cousin Julia Snell who introduced me as Minister Rosie Goldsby everywhere we went and told me I was going to walk in my gift as a minister.

Missionary Emma Lee Green who provided enough resources for me to study to show myself proficient in the study of the Word of God.

My "Sister Girl", Bessie Lee Vernell who helped me through my consecration period while shedding off all those things that would distract me from my calling.

Bobbie Smoots who believed in my calling and gave me my first opportunity to speak at the church she attended for Women's Day.

Bishop Everett Jefferson and Miles Goldsby, the first men who encouraged me to stay focused and follow the leading of the Holy Spirit.

Vandessea Lee, a godmother that left the church she attended so that she could join the church I pastored and provide support.

To the people who joined The Temple Non-Denominational Church and allowed me to be one of their pastors.

Pastor Ann McDonald, who was a listening ear, paid for my books while I was in school for my Master's Degree and gave me many opportunities to preach.

My daughter and friend Candace Pitts, a fellow minister of the gospel who was my study partner while achieving my Master's and Doctorate and contributed generously to the payment of my Doctorate degree.

My son's Paul, Sidney, Minister Daniel, and Malcohm who accepted me as their mother and minister. Congrats to Sidney who lived out his passion and published his first book.

My sister Madeline and brother Marvin who were not called to be ministers but listened and supported my ministry.

To Norris Watson who told me a play was not a book.

Printed in the United States
by Baker & Taylor Publisher Services